# This Is My
# School

by **Mark Weakland**                    illustrated by **Nina de Polonia-Nill**

PICTURE WINDOW BOOKS
a capstone imprint

# Khushi

Name: **Khushi**

Birthday: **February 7**

Favorite color: **pink**

Favorite food: **cheeseburgers**

Favorite animal: **cat**

I want to be a: **doctor**

# Table of Contents

# Inside My School

Hi, I'm Khushi, and this is my school! There are so many things to see, hear, and smell inside. We have rooms filled with books and computers. We also have special rooms for making music and art. There is a place to play sports and a place to eat lunch. Come on! Let's go exploring!

# The Office Buzz

Our first stop is the office. Phones ring. Bells ding. The copy machine hums nonstop. People buzz in and out all day. The principal works in the office. The office coordinators do too. Every phone call for the school comes through the office. So does every person who visits the building. The office is like a busy beehive!

# Time to Learn

Here's where I spend most of my day at school: my classroom. All classrooms are safe places for kids to learn. They have books, paper, and pencils. They have teachers who care about kids too! But classrooms also have things that make them different from each other. Some classrooms have beanbags and bouncy balls to sit on. Some have plants, fish, or class pets.

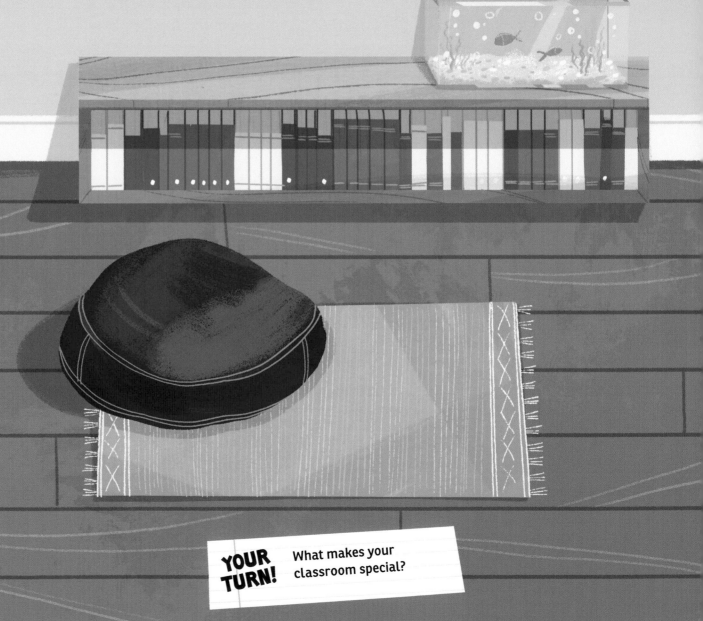

**YOUR TURN!** What makes your classroom special?

# Adjectives

How does it look, feel, smell, taste, sound?

The _____ bear is _____.

| | |
|---|---|
| brown | fuzzy |
| fat | sleepy |
| grumpy | loud |

# Books and More

The next stop is the library. Sometimes we call this place the media center. It has books, magazines, newspapers, e-books, and computers. Our librarian helps us find whatever we need. He seems to know everything about everything! We even have a makerspace in our library, where we all share ideas and work together.

**YOUR TURN!** What's your favorite part of the library and why?

11

# Let's Eat

After visiting the library and feeding our brains, it's time to feed our stomachs! We always have lots of good food to eat in the lunchroom. First we scan our meal card. Then we wait our turn in the serving area. I really like our servers. If I ask nicely, they give me extra peaches. Once our trays are full, we find a place to sit in the seating area. My friends and I make sure no one sits alone.

# Get Moving

*SQUEAK! TWEET! THUMP, THUMP, THUMP!* The gym is a big, noisy place with a tall ceiling and a wooden floor. It's filled with the sounds of tennis shoes, whistles, and bouncing balls. A gym is a place to play sports, such as basketball or volleyball. Gyms also hold concerts and assemblies. Our school mascot is painted on the gym wall. Go, Eagles!

**YOUR TURN!** If you were a gym teacher, what sport would you teach to others and why?

# Special Classrooms

Some classrooms are extra special. The art room is full of colorful paintings and drawings we've done. It smells like clay and markers. Next door is the music room. We sing and play instruments in there. We don't always sound the best, but we try hard. Down the hall is the computer room. It's really quiet. All you hear are whirring fans and clicking keys.

# Bathroom Break

What's one kind of room every school building has?
Bathrooms! All school bathrooms have toilets, sinks,
and air driers or paper towels. My school has a few
big bathrooms, with lots of stalls, and a few small
bathrooms. The small ones have just one toilet.
In some elementary schools, each classroom has
its own single-toilet bathroom.

# One Awesome School

That's it! That's my school! From the office to the gym, each room is special and important in its own way. When you put them all together, they make one awesome place for my friends and me to learn. But what's the best part of any school? The people in it!

**YOUR TURN!** What is your favorite room in your school and why?

21

# Glossary

**assembly**—a meeting of lots of people

**coordinator**—someone who makes sure things are in order and running smoothly

**makerspace**—a place where people gather to work on projects and share ideas, usually about computers or technology

**mascot**—a person or animal that stands for a school, sports team, or other group

**media**—a group of mediums that share messages, including TV, radio, and the Internet

**principal**—the head of a public school

**stall**—a small, closed-in space; bathroom stalls have a toilet inside them

**whirring**—a low, buzzing sound

## Read More

**O'Connell, Eleanor.** *Schools Around the World.* Adventures in Culture. New York: Gareth Stevens Publishing, 2017.

**Rissman, Rebecca.** *Going to School.* Comparing Past and Present. Chicago: Capstone Heinemann Library, 2014.

**Smith, Penny.** *A School Like Mine: A Celebration of Schools Around the World.* Children Just Like Me. New York: DK Publishing, 2016.

## Internet Sites

Use FactHound to find Internet sites related to this book.

Visit *www.facthound.com*

Just type in 9781515838517 and go.

## Critical Thinking Questions

1. What do you think would happen if a school didn't have a library? What if it didn't have an office or bathrooms?

2. The author says that the best part of any school is the people in it. What evidence does he give in this book to prove that statement? Use the text and illustrations to support your answer.

3. Are there rooms in your school that weren't shown in this book? What would you tell a friend about those rooms?

# Index

## Look for all the books in the series:

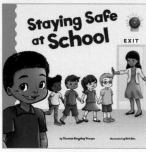

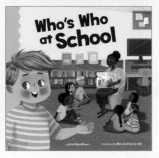

Special thanks to our adviser, Sara Hjelmeland, M.Ed., Kindergarten Teacher, for her expertise.

Editor: Jill Kalz
Designer: Lori Bye
Production Specialist: Laura Manthe
The illustrations in this book were created digitally.

Picture Window Books are published by Capstone
1710 Roe Crest Drive, North Mankato, Minnesota 56003
www.mycapstone.com

Library of Congress Cataloging-in-Publication Data is available on the Library of Congress website.
ISBN 978-1-5158-3851-7 (library binding)
ISBN 978-1-5158-4066-4 (paperback)
ISBN 978-1-5158-3857-9 (eBook PDF)
Summary: How do I find my way around school? *This Is My School* gives young readers the grand tour through all the rooms and special areas that make up an elementary-school building. Featuring playful illustrations that embrace diversity, and led by a 1st-person student narrator, the tour takes kids to the front office, the library, the gym, the nurse's office, and other rooms.

Shutterstock: jannoon028, (notebook) design element throughout

Printed in the United States    5669